Chapter 1: Intelligence and Espionage

Intelligence and espionage are two critical components of national security and international relations. Intelligence refers to the gathering, analyzing, and dissemination of information for decision-making purposes, while espionage specifically refers to the use of clandestine methods to gather information.

The historical evolution of these fields has played a critical role in shaping the course of history, from ancient civilizations to modern nation-states. In today's world, intelligence and espionage are more important than ever, as nations compete for power and influence in an increasingly interconnected and complex global system.

This book provides a comprehensive overview of intelligence and espionage tradecraft, including their historical evolution, their purpose and importance in today's world, and the techniques employed in each field. By understanding the methods and strategies employed by intelligence and espionage professionals, readers can gain a better understanding of the complex world of international relations and the role these fields play in shaping it.

Throughout the following chapters, readers will explore the various facets of intelligence and espionage tradecraft, from collection and analysis to counterintelligence and covert action. Whether you are a student of international relations, a professional in the field, or simply interested in learning more about these critical topics, this book will provide a comprehensive and informative overview of the world of intelligence and espionage.

Intelligence and espionage are two critical components of national security and international relations. While they are often used interchangeably, they are distinct fields with different methods and objectives.

Intelligence is defined as the gathering, analyzing, and dissemination of information for decision-making purposes. This information can come from a variety of sources, including open source materials, human sources, and technical means such as signals intelligence (SIGINT) or imagery intelligence (IMINT). The primary objective of intelligence is to provide decision-makers with accurate and timely information to help them make informed decisions.

Espionage, on the other hand, specifically refers to the use of clandestine methods to gather information. This can include recruiting human sources, conducting surveillance, or stealing information through cyberattacks or other means. The objective of espionage is to gather information that is not publicly available, often for strategic or military purposes.

While intelligence and espionage are distinct fields, they are often closely related. Many intelligence agencies, for example, employ both overt and covert methods to gather information.

Additionally, intelligence agencies often work closely with law enforcement agencies to gather information on criminal organizations or other threats.

Understanding the distinction between intelligence and espionage is critical for professionals in the field, as well as for policymakers and the general public. Intelligence is a critical tool for decision-making, while espionage can be an effective means of gathering information that is not publicly available. However, the use of espionage can also raise ethical and legal questions, particularly when it involves the violation of an individual's privacy or national sovereignty.

In the following sections, we will explore the historical evolution of intelligence and espionage, their importance in today's world, and the techniques and methods used in each field. By understanding the methods and strategies employed by intelligence and espionage professionals, readers can gain a better understanding of the complex world of international relations and the role these fields play in shaping it.

Intelligence has been a critical component of human history since ancient times. The earliest known use of intelligence can be traced back to the ancient Greeks, who used information gathered from spies to gain an advantage in battles and political negotiations. In China, the use of intelligence was formalized with the establishment of the "cangue" system in the Han Dynasty, which used government officials to gather and analyze information.

During the Middle Ages, intelligence gathering continued to play an important role in military and political affairs. The Catholic Church, for example, established a vast network of spies and informants to gather information on heretics and political rivals. Similarly, the feudal lords of Japan employed ninja as spies and assassins.

The modern era of Intelligence began in the late 19th century with the creation of the French intelligence agency, the Deuxième Bureau. Other countries quickly followed suit, with the British establishing the Secret Intelligence Service (SIS, also known as MI6) in 1909 and the Germans creating the Abwehr in 1921.

The First World War saw a significant increase in the use of intelligence, with both sides relying heavily on code-breaking and other forms of espionage. The Second World War saw an even greater reliance on intelligence, with the Allied code-breakers at Bletchley Park playing a critical role in defeating Nazi Germany.

In the post-World War II era, intelligence gathering became an even more important tool of national security and international relations. The Cold War saw a massive expansion of intelligence agencies and an increase in the use of covert operations. The United States, for example, conducted a series of covert operations in Latin America and other regions during this period, often in support of anti-communist forces.

The use of technology, including advanced satellites and sophisticated computer algorithms, has revolutionized the field of intelligence gathering. However, the basic methods and principles of intelligence gathering have remained largely unchanged, emphasizing the importance of human intelligence and the need for careful analysis and interpretation of information.

In today's world, intelligence gathering remains a critical tool for ensuring national security and promoting international relations. With the rise of global terrorism and the proliferation of weapons of mass destruction, intelligence agencies are more important than ever before.

Intelligence gathering is used to identify and track terrorist groups, to disrupt their operations and prevent attacks before they occur. The intelligence community also plays a key role in identifying and preventing the spread of weapons of mass destruction.

Intelligence is also critical for understanding the intentions and capabilities of other countries. In a world where economic and military power is increasingly important, accurate intelligence is essential for making informed decisions about trade, security, and foreign policy.

Moreover, intelligence gathering is critical for protecting human rights and promoting democracy around the world. By gathering information about human rights abuses and other forms of oppression, intelligence agencies can help to prevent violence and promote social justice.

In recent years, there has been a growing debate over the balance between national security and civil liberties. Critics argue that the increased use of surveillance and other intelligence-gathering techniques threatens individual privacy and civil liberties. Proponents of these techniques argue that they are necessary for ensuring national security in a dangerous and uncertain world.

Despite this debate, it is clear that intelligence gathering will continue to play a critical role in international affairs. The challenge for intelligence agencies will be to find the right balance between national security and civil liberties, while continuing to gather the information needed to protect their citizens and promote peace and prosperity around the world.

Intelligence and espionage are fields that are shrouded in secrecy and surrounded by controversy. The use of covert and often invasive techniques raises important ethical questions about the balance between national security and individual rights.

Intelligence agencies must operate within a framework of laws and regulations designed to protect civil liberties and human rights. The use of torture, for example, is prohibited by international law and is widely considered to be a violation of human rights. Other techniques, such as the use of drones for targeted killings, raise difficult ethical questions about the use of force and the protection of civilians. In addition, intelligence agencies must consider the potential for abuse of power, and the responsibility that comes with access to sensitive information.

The use of covert operations, surveillance, and other intelligence-gathering techniques can damage diplomatic relations and undermine trust between nations. The disclosure of classified information can also have serious consequences for national security and foreign policy. Intelligence agencies must balance the need for information with the potential impact on international relations.

The use of private contractors and other third parties can create additional ethical concerns. In recent years, the use of private military contractors and intelligence firms has raised questions about accountability and oversight. The actions of these third parties can reflect poorly on the government and damage diplomatic relations.

To address these ethical concerns, intelligence agencies must operate with transparency and oversight. Clear ethical guidelines and rigorous oversight mechanisms will be essential for ensuring that intelligence agencies operate within the bounds of democratic values and respect for human rights. Oversight mechanisms may include external review by independent panels, internal audits, and public reporting on agency activities.

The use of intelligence and espionage raises important ethical questions about the balance between national security and individual rights. Intelligence agencies must operate within a framework of laws and regulations designed to protect civil liberties and human rights. They must also consider the impact of their actions on international relations and the potential for abuse of power. Clear ethical guidelines and rigorous oversight mechanisms are essential for ensuring that intelligence agencies operate within the bounds of democratic values and respect for human rights.

Chapter 2: Intelligence Gathering Disciplines

Effective intelligence gathering is crucial to the success of any intelligence agency or operative. In this chapter, we will explore a variety of techniques used for gathering intelligence, including both traditional and modern methods.

HUMINT (Human Intelligence)

HUMINT involves the use of human sources to collect information. This can include recruiting spies, cultivating informants, and debriefing defectors. HUMINT is often considered the most valuable form of intelligence gathering due to the nuanced and contextual information that can be obtained through personal relationships and interactions.

Example: During the Cold War, the CIA recruited a high-ranking KGB officer named Oleg Penkovsky to serve as a spy for the United States. Penkovsky provided the US with valuable information about Soviet military capabilities and intentions, which helped to mitigate the risk of a nuclear confrontation.

SIGINT (Signals Intelligence)

SIGINT involves intercepting and analyzing electronic signals and communications, including radio and satellite transmissions, email, and internet traffic. SIGINT can be used to gather information about military capabilities, terrorist activities, and criminal organizations.

Example: The National Security Agency (NSA) is responsible for collecting and analyzing SIGINT. In the aftermath of the September 11th attacks, the NSA intercepted communications between Al-Qaeda operatives that provided crucial information about their plans and activities.

IMINT (Imagery Intelligence)

IMINT involves the collection and analysis of visual imagery, including photographs and satellite imagery. IMINT can be used to gather information about military capabilities, infrastructure, and natural resources.

Example: During the Cuban Missile Crisis, the US relied on IMINT to identify Soviet missile sites in Cuba. U-2 spy planes flew over Cuba and took photographs, which were used to confirm the presence of nuclear missiles and to plan a blockade of Cuba to prevent further Soviet missile shipments.

OSINT (Open Source Intelligence)

OSINT involves gathering information from publicly available sources, including news articles, social media, and government reports. OSINT can be used to gather information about individuals, organizations, and events.

Example: During the search for Osama bin Laden, the US used OSINT to track his movements and activities. By analyzing public statements made by Al-Qaeda operatives and monitoring their social media activity, the US was able to gather information about bin Laden's whereabouts and ultimately locate and kill him.

Chapter 3: The Intelligence Cycle

The intelligence cycle is the fundamental process that drives intelligence agencies and their efforts to collect, analyze, and disseminate information. It is a complex and dynamic system that requires careful coordination and execution at each stage. From the collection of raw data to the dissemination of actionable intelligence, the intelligence cycle is a crucial tool in the arsenal of any intelligence agency. In this chapter, we will explore the intricacies of the intelligence cycle, examining each stage in detail and providing examples of how these stages play out in real-world intelligence operations. By the end of this chapter, you will have a thorough understanding of how the intelligence cycle works and how it can be used to gather, analyze, and act upon information to further national security interests.

Part 1: Planning and Direction

The first stage of the intelligence cycle is planning and direction. This is where intelligence agencies determine the specific information they need to gather and analyze, and how they will go about doing so. This stage involves setting intelligence priorities, identifying intelligence requirements, and allocating resources to meet those requirements.

In order to determine intelligence priorities, agencies must consider a wide range of factors, such as the threat environment, political climate, and national security objectives. Once these priorities have been established, intelligence requirements are identified. These are specific pieces of information that are needed to support national security interests, such as the intentions of foreign governments, the capabilities of terrorist organizations, or the movements of military forces.

Once intelligence requirements have been identified, resources are allocated to meet them. This involves determining the appropriate collection methods, such as human intelligence (HUMINT), signals intelligence (SIGINT), or imagery intelligence (IMINT). It also involves determining the appropriate sources and methods for collecting the necessary information.

Effective planning and direction is crucial for the success of the intelligence cycle. It ensures that resources are used efficiently and effectively, and that intelligence agencies are able to gather the information necessary to support national security objectives.

The second stage of the intelligence cycle is collection. This is where intelligence agencies collect information from a wide range of sources and methods, including open source materials, human sources, technical sources, and others.

Open source collection involves gathering information from publicly available sources such as newspapers, magazines, television and radio broadcasts, and the internet. This type of collection is important because it can provide a wealth of information that is readily available to anyone with access to these sources.

Human intelligence (HUMINT) collection involves the use of human sources, such as agents or informants, to gather information. This type of collection is often the most difficult and dangerous, as it involves establishing and maintaining relationships with individuals who may be hostile to the intelligence agency's objectives.

Technical collection involves the use of advanced technology, such as satellite imagery and signals intelligence (SIGINT), to gather information. This type of collection can provide highly detailed and valuable information, but it requires sophisticated technology and specialized expertise to use effectively.

Collection is a critical stage in the intelligence cycle, as it provides the raw data needed to generate intelligence. However, collecting information can be challenging, as it often requires significant resources and the use of sensitive methods that may be subject to detection or interception by adversaries. Effective collection requires careful planning, strong operational security measures, and the ability to adapt quickly to changing circumstances.

Part 3: Processing and Exploitation

Once information has been collected, it must be processed and analyzed to identify relevant intelligence. This is the third stage of the intelligence cycle, known as processing and exploitation.

During this stage, intelligence analysts review and evaluate the information collected during the previous stage. They assess the accuracy, reliability, and relevance of the information and determine how it fits into the larger intelligence picture.

Analysts also work to identify any patterns or trends in the information, as well as any gaps or inconsistencies. They may use data analytics and other tools to help identify key insights and generate new intelligence.

Processing and exploitation is a critical stage in the intelligence cycle, as it is where the raw data is transformed into usable intelligence. However, this stage can be complex and time-consuming, particularly if the information collected is large in volume or diverse in nature.

Effective processing and exploitation requires skilled analysts with specialized knowledge and expertise. It also requires the use of advanced technology and tools to help manage and analyze large amounts of data. Finally, it requires careful coordination and communication between different parts of the intelligence organization to ensure that intelligence is processed and exploited effectively and efficiently.

Part 4: Analysis and Production

After the information has been processed and exploited, it is time to analyze the data and produce intelligence. This is the fourth stage of the intelligence cycle, known as analysis and production.

During this stage, intelligence analysts use a variety of techniques and methods to analyze the information collected during the previous stages. They seek to understand the meaning behind the data and to identify potential threats, opportunities, or other important insights.

Analysts may use a variety of tools and methods, including statistical analysis, geospatial analysis, network analysis, and others. They may also use structured analytic techniques such as brainstorming, red teaming, and alternative futures analysis to generate new insights.

Once the analysis is complete, the intelligence is produced in a format that is suitable for dissemination to decision-makers. This may include written reports, briefings, or other forms of communication.

Effective analysis and production require skilled analysts who are able to synthesize large amounts of data and identify key insights. It also requires the use of advanced technology and tools to support analysis and production, as well as strong communication and collaboration skills to ensure that the intelligence is disseminated effectively.

Part 5: Dissemination and Feedback

The final stage of the intelligence cycle is dissemination and feedback. In this stage, the intelligence produced in the previous stages is shared with those who need it, such as policymakers, military commanders, or law enforcement agencies.

Dissemination can take many forms, including written reports, oral briefings, or online platforms. The intelligence community may also use more targeted methods of dissemination, such as sharing information with specific agencies or officials.

Effective dissemination requires careful consideration of the audience and their specific needs. The intelligence must be presented in a way that is easily understood and relevant to the recipient. It is also important to ensure that the intelligence is disseminated securely and that appropriate measures are taken to protect sensitive information.

Feedback is an important component of the dissemination process. Decision-makers may provide feedback on the intelligence they receive, which can help to refine the collection, analysis, and production processes in future intelligence cycles.

Feedback can also come from other sources, such as intelligence consumers who identify gaps or areas where the intelligence could be improved. This feedback is used to inform ongoing improvements to the intelligence process, ensuring that it remains relevant and effective in an ever-changing global landscape.

The dissemination and feedback stage ensures that the intelligence produced in the previous stages is shared with those who need it and that feedback is received to improve the intelligence process.

Chapter 4: Covert Communication techniques

Covert communication refers to any method of transmitting information that is hidden or disguised in some way. This can include everything from secret codes and ciphers, to invisible ink and covert signaling. In intelligence and espionage operations, the ability to communicate covertly is essential for maintaining secrecy and avoiding detection.

The use of covert communication techniques dates back thousands of years, with examples found in ancient civilizations such as Greece and Rome. However, the development of modern encryption techniques during World War II marked a major turning point in the field of covert communication, and today there are countless methods available for transmitting information in a covert manner.

Some common types of covert communication techniques include steganography, which involves hiding information within another file or image, and cryptography, which involves scrambling the contents of a message using a secret key. Other techniques include microdots, which are tiny dots of text that can be hidden in plain sight, and dead drops, which involve leaving a message in a secret location for another person to retrieve.

In the rest of this chapter we will explore some of these techniques in more detail:

Technique: Steganography

Steganography is the practice of hiding secret information within a non-secret message in such a way that it cannot be easily detected or interpreted. Here is a step-by-step guide to implementing steganography in your covert communication:

Choose a cover message: The first step is to choose a cover message that you will use to hide your secret information. This could be anything from a plain text message to a photograph or audio file.

Select your steganography software: There are several steganography software tools available online that you can use to embed your secret message within your cover message. Some popular options include OpenStego, SilentEye, and Steghide.

Embed your secret message: Using your steganography software of choice, embed your secret message within your cover message. This will typically involve selecting the cover message and the secret message, specifying any encryption or compression options you want to use, and then embedding the secret message within the cover message.

Transmit the message: Once you have embedded your secret message within your cover message, you can transmit it to your intended recipient using any communication channel you choose (e.g. email, instant messaging, social media, etc.).

Extract the secret message: To extract the secret message from the cover message, the recipient will need to use the same steganography software that you used to embed the message. They will typically need to specify the location of the cover message and provide any necessary decryption or password information to extract the secret message.

It Is important to note that steganography is not foolproof and there are ways to detect the presence of hidden messages, particularly if the cover message has been altered in any way. Therefore, it is important to use additional encryption and security measures to protect your information.

Technique: Invisible Ink

Invisible ink is a method of covert communication that involves hiding a message within a seemingly innocuous substance that can only be revealed through the use of a specific reagent or method.

Materials:

Lemon juice or baking soda solution

Cotton swab or paintbrush

White paper or cardstock

Heat source (optional)

Steps:

Mix lemon juice or baking soda with water to create a solution.

Use a cotton swab or paintbrush to write a message onto the paper using the solution. Be sure to apply the solution liberally to ensure that the message is visible when revealed.
Allow the solution to dry completely.

To reveal the message, hold the paper over a heat source such as a light bulb or candle flame. The heat will cause the message to darken and become visible. Alternatively, you can also use a different reagent such as iodine or vinegar to reveal the message.

Tips:

Use a blank piece of paper as the cover page for the message to avoid suspicion.

Use a font size and style that can be easily read when revealed.

Make sure the paper is completely dry before attempting to reveal the message.

Store the solution in a container that is labeled as something else, such as "lemon juice for cooking" to avoid suspicion.

Applications:

Invisible ink can be used to pass secret messages in plain sight, such as in letters, books, or notes.

It can also be used as a method of authentication, such as marking items with an invisible ink stamp to verify their authenticity.

Limitations:

The message is only visible when the reagent or method is used, so the recipient must know how to reveal the message.

The message can be accidentally revealed if it comes into contact with moisture or other substances that react with the solution.

Invisible ink is not a foolproof method of communication and should be used in combination with other covert communication techniques for maximum security.

Practice Exercise:

Practice creating and revealing an invisible ink message using lemon juice or baking soda solution.

Try using different reagents such as vinegar or iodine to reveal the message.

Think of a scenario where invisible ink could be used as a method of covert communication and write a message using the technique.

Technique: Dead drops

Dead drops are a way of leaving and retrieving messages or other materials at a pre-arranged location without needing to meet in person. This technique can be useful for communicating with someone who is difficult to reach or for exchanging sensitive information without the risk of detection.

To use a dead drop for communication, follow these steps:

Identify a location for the dead drop. This should be a public location that is easy for both parties to access, but not so well-traveled that the materials will be accidentally discovered. Examples of good locations might include a park bench, a public restroom stall, or a hidden alcove in a public building.

Create a container for the message or materials. This could be a small plastic bag, a hollowed-out book, or any other object that can be left inconspicuously in the chosen location.

Prepare the message or materials. Make sure they are securely packaged and protected from the elements if necessary. If you are leaving a message, consider using a code or cipher to make it more difficult for unauthorized parties to understand.

Place the container in the dead drop location. Make sure it is well-hidden and inconspicuous so that it won't attract attention.

Notify the other party that the message or materials are waiting in the dead drop. This could be done through a pre-arranged code or signal, or by simply sending a message through another means of communication.

Retrieve the message or materials from the dead drop. Be careful not to arouse suspicion while doing so, and make sure to leave the location undisturbed so that others will not discover the dead drop.

Dead drops can be a highly effective means of covert communication when used properly. However, it is important to take precautions to avoid detection, such as using multiple dead drops to reduce the risk of surveillance, and avoiding conspicuous behavior when retrieving messages.

Technique: Ciphertext

Ciphertext is the practice of converting plain text into a secret code that can be transmitted through communication channels without revealing the message's content. It involves the use of encryption algorithms to convert the original message into an unreadable format. The message is then transmitted to the recipient, who uses decryption techniques to convert the ciphertext back to plain text.

Ciphertext techniques have been used for centuries to protect sensitive information, such as military secrets and diplomatic communications. The technique is still widely used today in various fields, including cybersecurity, banking, and government communications.

To use ciphertext, one must first select an encryption algorithm. These algorithms can range from simple substitution ciphers to more complex block ciphers or stream ciphers. The encryption algorithm will determine the level of security and complexity of the ciphertext.

Once an encryption algorithm is selected, the plaintext message is converted into ciphertext using the algorithm. This can be done manually, but there are also computer programs and online tools available to make the process easier.

The ciphertext message is then transmitted to the recipient using a secure communication channel. The recipient will use a decryption algorithm and a secret key to convert the ciphertext back into plaintext. It is important to note that the decryption algorithm must match the encryption algorithm used to create the ciphertext, and the secret key must be kept secure to maintain the confidentiality of the message.

One of the most common examples of ciphertext is the Advanced Encryption Standard (AES), which is used by the U.S. government to protect classified information. Another example is the RSA algorithm, which is widely used in online transactions to secure data transmission.

In conclusion, ciphertext is a powerful covert communication technique that can be used to protect sensitive information. By using encryption algorithms and secure communication channels, plaintext messages can be converted into unreadable ciphertext, ensuring that only the

intended recipient can access the original
message.

Technique: Caesar cipher

A Caesar cipher is one of the simplest and most
widely known encryption techniques. It is a type of
substitution cipher in which each letter in the
plaintext is shifted a certain number of places
down the alphabet. For example, with a shift of 3,
A would be replaced by D, B would become E, and
so on.

To use a Caesar cipher, one first chooses a shift
value. This can be any number between 1 and 25,
representing the number of places each letter will
be shifted. Then, each letter in the plaintext is
replaced by the letter that is shifted by the chosen
number of places.

For example, with a shift of 3:

Plaintext: THE QUICK BROWN FOX JUMPS OVER THE LAZY DOG

Ciphertext: WKH TXLFN EURZQ IRA MXPSV RYHU WKH ODCB GRJ

In this example, each letter in the plaintext has been shifted three places down the alphabet. So, T becomes W, H becomes K, and so on.

The Caesar cipher is easily broken and not secure against modern cryptographic analysis. However, it can be a useful tool for simple and quick encryption in certain situations. It is often used as a stepping stone for teaching more complex encryption methods.

Technique: The Playfair cipher

The Playfair Cipher was invented in 1854 by Charles Wheatstone, but was named after his friend and fellow inventor, Lyon Playfair. This cipher is a polygraphic substitution cipher, which means that it substitutes groups of letters instead of individual letters.

The Playfair Cipher uses a 5x5 grid of letters, which includes all 26 letters of the alphabet except for "Q". The key is a keyword or phrase, which is used to populate the grid. The letters of the key are inserted into the grid in order, and then the remaining letters of the alphabet are filled in order, omitting "Q".

To encrypt a message using the Playfair Cipher, the plaintext is divided into pairs of letters. If there is an odd number of letters, a dummy letter (such as "X") is added to the end to make an even number. Each pair of letters is then encrypted using the following steps:

If the two letters are the same, add an "X" between them.
Find the positions of the two letters in the grid.

If the letters are in the same row, replace them with the letters to their right (wrapping around to the beginning of the row if necessary).

If the letters are in the same column, replace them with the letters below them (wrapping around to the top of the column if necessary).

If the letters are not in the same row or column, replace each letter with the letter in the same row and the other letter's column.

To decrypt a message using the Playfair Cipher, the inverse of the encryption process is used. The ciphertext is divided into pairs of letters, and the position of each letter in the grid is found. If the letters are in the same row or column, they are replaced with the letter to their left or above, respectively. If the letters are not in the same row or column, each letter is replaced with the letter in the same row and the other letter's column.

The Playfair Cipher Is more secure than some other simple substitution ciphers, but it is still vulnerable to cryptanalysis. For example, if an attacker knows that a certain word or phrase appears in the plaintext, they can look for patterns in the ciphertext to try to determine the key. However, if used properly and with a strong key, the Playfair Cipher can be a useful tool for covert communication.

Technique: The Vigenère cipher

The Vigenère cipher is a polyalphabetic substitution cipher, which means that it uses multiple substitution alphabets. Unlike the Caesar cipher, which is a monoalphabetic cipher and uses only one substitution alphabet, the Vigenère cipher uses a different substitution alphabet for each letter of the plaintext.

To use the Vigenère cipher, you first need to choose a keyword, which can be any word or phrase. Let's say we choose the keyword "LEMON". You then repeat the keyword over and over until it is at least as long as the plaintext you want to encrypt. So if your plaintext is "ATTACK AT

DAWN", you would repeat the keyword to get "LEMONLEMONLE".

Next, you write the plaintext underneath the repeated keyword, like this:

Copy code

LEMONLEMONLE

ATTACKATDAWN

To encrypt each letter of the plaintext, you find the row corresponding to the letter of the keyword, and the column corresponding to the letter of the plaintext. The letter at the intersection of the row and column is the ciphertext letter. So to encrypt the first letter "A", you would find the row for "L" (the first letter of the keyword) and the column for "A" (the first letter of the plaintext), and find the letter at their intersection, which is "L". Continuing in this way, you can encrypt the entire plaintext:

Makefile

Copy code

Plaintext: ATTACK AT DAWN

Keyword: LEMON LEMON LE

Ciphertext: LXFOPVEFRNHR

To decrypt the ciphertext, you use the same keyword and the same process, but instead of finding the ciphertext letter at the intersection of the row and column, you find the plaintext letter at the intersection.

Technique: Live drop

Live drops are a method of covert communication in which two agents communicate without ever meeting each other. Unlike dead drops, where information is left in a specific location to be retrieved at a later time, live drops involve the exchange of information in real-time.

Live drops require two agents who are in the same physical location but must not have direct contact with each other. This method is often used when agents are under surveillance or when meeting in person is too risky.

The simplest form of a live drop is a prearranged signal between the two agents. The signal can be something as simple as a hand gesture or a code phrase. The two agents must be in a location where they can observe each other without arousing suspicion.

Another form of a live drop is a brush pass. This involves one agent passing an object to another while in public. The object could be anything from a briefcase to a shopping bag. This method requires the two agents to be walking in opposite directions, and the object is passed between them as they walk past each other.

Live drops can also be performed using electronic devices, such as a mobile phone. In this case, the two agents can use a prearranged code to communicate with each other without arousing suspicion. For example, the agent could send a text message that appears to be an innocent message to a friend, but the message actually contains information for the other agent.

In conclusion, live drops are a useful technique for covert communication when direct contact is not possible or too risky. They require careful planning and prearranged signals, but when executed correctly, live drops can be an effective way for two agents to exchange information without detection.

Technique: Microdot

Microdot is a form of steganography that involves hiding small, high-resolution images on documents or other surfaces. The microdots are usually no larger than a period at the end of a sentence and can be difficult to detect without the use of specialized equipment.

Microdots are commonly used in espionage and intelligence operations as a way to transmit secret information. For example, a spy might photograph a classified document using a high-resolution camera, then reduce the image to the size of a microdot and hide it on a seemingly innocuous item, such as a postage stamp.

To read a microdot, a special microscope is needed to enlarge the image. In the past, this required physical access to the object containing the microdot, but with modern technology, it is possible to read microdots remotely using high-powered cameras and software.

One famous example of the use of microdots in espionage was the case of Rudolf Abel, a Soviet spy who was arrested in the United States in 1957. Abel had been using microdots to communicate with his handlers, and his arrest led to the discovery of a number of microdots hidden on various objects in his possession.

Microdots are a highly effective form of covert communication, as they are difficult to detect and can be hidden in plain sight. However, they do require specialized equipment to read, which can be a drawback in some situations.

Technique: Covert Signaling

Covert signaling is the use of a pre-agreed system of signals between two or more individuals, in order to communicate in a way that is difficult for others to detect or understand. This technique is often used in situations where it is not possible to speak or write in a conventional manner, such as during covert operations or in hostile environments.

There are many different types of covert signals that can be used, depending on the situation and the individuals involved. Some examples of covert signals include:

Hand signals: These are often used in military operations or when individuals need to communicate in silence. For example, a raised hand might indicate that it is safe to move forward, while a lowered hand might indicate that it is not safe.

Clothing signals: This involves wearing clothing or accessories that have a specific meaning, such as a particular color or pattern. For example, a red scarf might indicate that a particular location is dangerous, while a blue hat might indicate that it is safe.

Sound signals: These can include whistles, clicks, or other sounds that have a specific meaning. For example, one whistle might mean "move forward," while two whistles might mean "retreat."

Visual signals: These can include flashing lights, mirrors, or other visual cues. For example, a flashlight might be used to signal a specific location or to indicate the need for assistance.

Covert signaling can be an effective way to communicate in situations where other methods are not possible or safe. However, it requires careful planning and coordination between the individuals involved in order to ensure that the signals are understood and that they do not attract unwanted attention.

Technique: Encrypted apps

Encrypted text apps and email services have become increasingly popular in recent years as a means of secure communication. These tools are designed to protect the privacy and security of messages exchanged between parties, making them an attractive option for individuals and organizations seeking to keep their conversations confidential.

Encrypted text apps, such as Signal and WhatsApp, use end-to-end encryption to secure messages. This means that messages are encrypted on the sender's device and can only be decrypted by the intended recipient's device. This makes it virtually impossible for anyone else to intercept and read the messages, including the app provider themselves. Similarly, encrypted email services, such as ProtonMail and Tutanota, use end-to-end encryption to secure email messages. This means that the email is encrypted on the sender's device and can only be decrypted by the intended recipient's device, ensuring that no one else can access the contents of the email.

These encrypted communication tools provide a secure way for individuals and organizations to communicate sensitive information without the risk of interception or eavesdropping. However, it is important to note that while these tools provide a high level of security, they are not foolproof. It is still possible for an attacker to gain access to a user's device and read their messages or emails, so it is important to take additional precautions, such as using strong passwords and two-factor authentication, to further protect sensitive communications.

Chapter 5: OSINT

OSINT, or Open Source Intelligence, is a term used to describe the collection and analysis of information that is publicly available. It includes any information that can be legally and ethically gathered from sources such as newspapers, social media, government reports, and online databases. OSINT is becoming increasingly important in today's world because of the vast amount of information that is available on the Internet.

OSINT has a wide range of applications, including law enforcement, military intelligence, corporate intelligence, and journalism. In each of these fields, OSINT can be used to gather information about individuals, organizations, and events. It can also be used to identify potential threats and to monitor trends and patterns.

The benefits of OSINT are many. For one, it is a cost-effective way to gather information, as it does not require the same level of resources as other forms of intelligence gathering. It is also a way to gather information that might be difficult or impossible to obtain through other means. Finally, OSINT can be used to verify information that has been obtained through other sources.

OSINT is not without its challenges, however. One of the biggest challenges is the sheer volume of information that is available. Sorting through this information can be a time-consuming and labor-intensive process. In addition, the quality of the information that is available can vary widely, and it can be difficult to verify the accuracy of the information that has been gathered.

Despite these challenges, OSINT is a valuable tool for anyone who needs to gather information quickly and efficiently. In the following sections, we will explore some of the key techniques and tools that are used in OSINT, and we will discuss how to use them effectively.

Once you have defined your research goals, the next step is to collect information. This involves gathering data from various sources, such as online databases, social media, news articles, and government records. The aim is to gather as much relevant information as possible to support your research goals.

There are different methods for collecting information in OSINT. One method is to use automated tools, such as web crawlers and data scrapers. These tools help to collect information from websites, social media platforms, and other sources automatically. Another method is to conduct manual searches on search engines, social media, and other online platforms. In this case, the researcher uses advanced search techniques to find relevant information.

It's essential to evaluate the reliability of the sources of information before using them. This is because some sources may be biased or provide false information. To ensure the accuracy of the information, it's important to cross-check and verify the information from multiple sources.

Social media has become a powerful source of information for OSINT practitioners. Almost everyone has a social media account, and they often share personal information, thoughts, and opinions publicly. By analyzing social media profiles and posts, an OSINT practitioner can gain valuable insights into a person's interests, beliefs, connections, and activities.

To perform social media analysis, an OSINT practitioner needs to identify the social media platforms that the target uses and locate their profiles. They can search for the target's name, username, email address, phone number, or other identifying information on various social media platforms. Once the target's profiles are located, the practitioner can examine their posts, comments, likes, followers, and friends.

Social media analysis can reveal a wealth of information about a target's personal and professional life. For example, a target's Facebook profile may indicate their education, job history, hobbies, relationship status, and political views. A target's Twitter feed may reveal their opinions on current events, their favorite news sources, and the people they follow. Instagram posts may provide insight into a target's lifestyle, travel habits, and social circle.

However, it's important to note that social media analysis also has limitations. Not all targets use social media, and some may use it very sparingly or may have strict privacy settings. Moreover, social media posts can be misleading, exaggerated, or outright false, so it's crucial to verify any information obtained through social media analysis with other sources.

Once you have identified your sources, the next step is to collect the relevant information. This can be done by using various tools and techniques, such as search engines, social media platforms, and other publicly available databases.

Some of the popular search engines that can be used for collecting OSINT include Google, Bing, and Yahoo. These search engines provide a wealth of information that can be used to collect data on a particular subject.

Social media platforms such as Facebook, Twitter, Instagram, and LinkedIn can also be used to gather information on an individual or organization. These platforms provide a wealth of information that can be used to build a profile of a person or organization, including their interests, connections, and affiliations.

Other publicly available databases, such as government databases, can also be used to collect OSINT. These databases provide information on various subjects, including criminal records, financial information, and property records.

It Is important to note that while collecting information, it is essential to verify the accuracy of the data collected. Information found through OSINT sources should be corroborated with other sources to ensure its accuracy and reliability.

Once you've collected all of your information, the next step is to analyze and correlate it to create a full picture of the situation or target you are investigating. This involves identifying patterns, relationships, and trends in the data you have collected.

There are several tools and techniques that can aid in the analysis and correlation process. These include:

Data visualization: This involves presenting your data in a visual format such as charts, graphs, or maps to help identify patterns and relationships that may not be immediately apparent in raw data.

Link analysis: This technique involves identifying relationships between different pieces of data such as people, organizations, and events to help build a comprehensive picture of a situation.

Pattern analysis: This technique involves identifying recurring patterns in data, such as specific behaviors or actions, to help identify trends or predict future behavior.

Text analysis: This involves using software to analyze large amounts of text data such as social media posts, news articles, or email correspondence to identify trends, sentiment, or key topics.

Geographic information systems (GIS): This involves using mapping tools to analyze and correlate geographic data to help identify patterns or relationships in physical locations.

Open-source intelligence tools: There are several software tools available that can assist in the analysis and correlation of OSINT data, such as Maltego, Palantir, and IBM i2 Analyst's Notebook.

It's Important to note that the analysis and correlation process requires careful consideration and critical thinking. It's essential to ensure that any conclusions drawn are based on solid evidence and that there is no bias or preconceptions influencing your analysis.

The analysis and correlation of OSINT data are critical components of the intelligence cycle. They enable you to create a comprehensive picture of a target or situation and make informed decisions based on the available information.

While OSINT can be a powerful tool for gathering information, it is important to recognize and consider the ethical implications of using it. The very nature of OSINT involves gathering information about individuals, organizations, and other entities without their knowledge or consent, which can potentially be invasive and unethical if not done carefully and responsibly.

Some key ethical considerations when using OSINT include:

Respect for privacy: It is important to respect individuals' privacy and not to collect or use information that is considered private or personal without their explicit consent. This includes avoiding collecting sensitive information such as medical or financial records, and being careful not to infringe on the privacy rights of individuals who are not directly related to the information being sought.

Use of information: The information gathered through OSINT should only be used for legitimate and lawful purposes. It is important to consider the potential consequences of using the information, and to ensure that it is not used in a way that could harm individuals or organizations.

Transparency: It is important to be transparent about the use of OSINT and to clearly communicate the purpose and methods of information gathering. This includes being upfront about the sources of information and how it will be used.

Accuracy and verification: OSINT information should be verified and validated to ensure accuracy and to prevent the spread of false information. It is important to rely on reputable sources and to cross-check information from multiple sources to ensure accuracy.

Respect for boundaries: It is important to respect legal and ethical boundaries when using OSINT, and to avoid crossing into areas that may be considered illegal or unethical. This includes avoiding activities such as hacking, social engineering, or other forms of cybercrime.

Overall, it is important to approach OSINT with a sense of responsibility and awareness of the ethical implications of using it. By respecting privacy, using information ethically and transparently, verifying accuracy, and respecting boundaries, OSINT can be a valuable tool for gathering information in a responsible and ethical manner.

Chapter 6: HUMINT

Human Intelligence, or HUMINT, refers to the collection of information through direct contact with individuals who possess the information. This information could be obtained through a variety of methods, including interviews, debriefings, elicitation, and other interpersonal communication techniques. HUMINT is a valuable tool for intelligence agencies as it can provide insight into a wide range of topics including political, economic, military, and social issues.

HUMINT techniques involve gathering information through face-to-face interactions with individuals who may have access to valuable intelligence. This type of intelligence gathering requires a certain level of interpersonal skills and the ability to establish trust and rapport with the individuals being interviewed. The information gathered can provide valuable insights into a target's plans, motivations, and intentions.

There are several types of HUMINT techniques, including overt and covert methods. Overt HUMINT involves collecting information through publicly available sources, such as interviews with government officials or attending public events. Covert HUMINT involves gathering information through clandestine methods, such as the use of undercover agents or the cultivation of human sources within an organization.

It is important to note that HUMINT collection is subject to legal and ethical constraints, and intelligence agencies must ensure that the information gathering process is conducted in a manner consistent with applicable laws and regulations. Furthermore, intelligence agencies must balance the potential benefits of HUMINT collection with the potential risks to the safety and security of individuals involved in the process.

Open-ended questions are an important HUMINT technique used to extract information from a source. These types of questions encourage the source to give a detailed answer and often provide more insight into their thoughts, feelings, and experiences. Open-ended questions are typically structured in a way that allows the source to provide a detailed response, without feeling constrained by a yes or no answer.

One of the advantages of open-ended questions is that they allow the interviewer to gain a better understanding of the source's perspective, attitudes, and motivations. This information can be valuable in developing a comprehensive understanding of the source's behavior, beliefs, and intentions.

Examples of open-ended questions include:

Can you tell me more about that?

What led you to that conclusion?

How did you feel about that situation?

It is important to note that open-ended questions should be used in conjunction with other techniques to establish credibility, build rapport, and avoid any misunderstandings that could hinder the intelligence gathering process.

Developing human intelligence sources is a critical aspect of HUMINT operations. In order to gather information effectively, HUMINT personnel must cultivate a network of reliable sources who can provide accurate and timely information. This requires a careful and strategic approach that includes identifying potential sources, establishing relationships, and building trust.

One of the key strategies for developing human intelligence sources is to focus on building personal relationships. HUMINT personnel must be able to establish rapport with potential sources, and to build trust over time through ongoing interactions. This may involve engaging in casual conversation, providing assistance or support, or other activities that help to establish a connection.

In addition to building relationships, HUMINT personnel must also be able to identify potential sources of information. This may involve conducting research and analysis to identify individuals or groups who may have access to relevant information, as well as assessing their reliability and credibility.

Once potential sources have been identified, HUMINT personnel must take steps to approach them and initiate a relationship. This may involve using intermediaries, such as trusted individuals who can introduce the HUMINT personnel to the potential source, or it may involve more direct approaches.

Regardless of the approach used, HUMINT personnel must be careful to protect the identity and safety of their sources. This may involve using code names or other methods to ensure anonymity, as well as taking steps to safeguard information that could be used to identify the source.

Ultimately, the success of HUMINT operations depends on the ability of personnel to cultivate and maintain relationships with reliable sources. This requires a long-term and sustained effort, and it may take months or even years to establish a robust network of human intelligence sources. However, the insights and information that can be gained through effective HUMINT operations can be invaluable for a wide range of national security and intelligence purposes.

Recruitment of sources is a crucial aspect of HUMINT collection, and it involves identifying and developing relationships with individuals who have access to valuable information. These individuals may be willing or unwilling to share information, and it is the job of the HUMINT collector to establish a rapport with them and persuade them to provide information.

Recruitment can be a delicate and time-consuming process, and it requires skill and sensitivity to navigate successfully. HUMINT collectors must use a range of techniques to recruit sources, including:

Building trust: HUMINT collectors must establish a relationship of trust with potential sources, and this can be achieved by showing a genuine interest in the source's concerns and needs.

Providing incentives: HUMINT collectors may offer incentives to sources in exchange for information. These incentives may be financial, such as cash payments, or non-financial, such as promises of protection or assistance.

Leveraging relationships: HUMINT collectors may use existing relationships to gain access to potential sources. For example, a collector may befriend a source's friend or family member in order to gain their trust and eventually gain access to the source.

Exploiting vulnerabilities: HUMINT collectors may identify and exploit a source's vulnerabilities, such as financial or personal problems, in order to persuade them to provide information.

Recruiting sources is a complex process that requires HUMINT collectors to be skilled at building relationships, identifying vulnerabilities, and offering incentives. Successful recruitment can provide valuable information and insights that would be impossible to obtain through other means.

Social engineering is a technique used to manipulate people to obtain information or access that would not be otherwise available. This can be done in a variety of ways, such as through impersonation, pretexting, or phishing.

Impersonation involves pretending to be someone else in order to gain trust and access to sensitive information. For example, a HUMINT operative may impersonate a repairman to gain entry into a building to plant surveillance equipment.

Pretexting is a technique where the operative creates a false identity or story in order to gain the target's trust and access to information. For example, a HUMINT operative may pose as a journalist to interview a target and obtain information.

Phishing is a technique that involves sending emails or messages that appear to be from a trustworthy source in order to obtain sensitive information. For example, a HUMINT operative may send an email posing as a bank and ask the target to provide their account information.

Social engineering can be a powerful HUMINT technique, but it requires a high level of skill and caution to avoid detection. Additionally, it can be unethical and potentially illegal if used improperly.

Elicitation is the process of obtaining information from a source through a planned and deliberate conversation. This technique involves building rapport with the source, gaining their trust, and subtly steering the conversation towards the desired information. Skilled elicitors use open-ended questions and active listening techniques to draw out the information without arousing suspicion or revealing their true intentions. It is important to note that elicitation should be conducted legally and ethically, with respect for the individual's privacy and rights.

Elicitation can be used in a variety of settings, from casual conversations to formal interviews. It is often employed in investigations and intelligence gathering operations, as well as in business and negotiation scenarios. Elicitation can be a powerful tool for obtaining critical information, but it requires a high level of interpersonal skill and a thorough understanding of the subject matter. It is also important to approach elicitation with caution and to be mindful of the potential risks and consequences.

Chapter 7: Agent Recruitment

Agent recruiting is the process of identifying, approaching, and persuading individuals to provide information or perform activities on behalf of an organization. It is an essential element of human intelligence gathering and is employed by governments, corporations, and other entities. Successful agent recruitment requires a combination of interpersonal skills, psychological insight, and operational planning.

The first step In the agent recruiting process is identifying potential candidates. This can be done through a variety of means, including open-source research, targeted networking, and insider knowledge. Once potential candidates have been identified, they must be assessed for their suitability as agents. This involves evaluating their access to information, reliability, motivation, and susceptibility to recruitment.

It Is important to note that agent recruitment is a delicate and often high-risk endeavor. Successful agents can provide valuable information and operational opportunities, but their exposure can also lead to significant damage to the recruiting organization. As a result, it is essential to carefully evaluate the potential benefits and risks of each recruitment opportunity and to follow established protocols to minimize the risks involved.

Before recruiting an agent, it's important to identify potential candidates who might be able to provide useful information or assistance. This can be done through various methods, including:

Networking: Building a network of contacts within the target organization or community can help identify individuals who may be willing to provide information or assistance.

Social media: Social media platforms can provide a wealth of information about individuals, including their interests, affiliations, and connections. This information can be used to identify potential recruits.

Open source research: Publicly available information, such as news articles, public records, and online directories, can be used to identify potential recruits.

Human intelligence sources: Existing agents or other sources of information can provide leads on potential recruits. It's important to carefully vet any information provided by sources to ensure their reliability.

Once potential candidates have been identified, a thorough assessment should be conducted to determine their suitability as agents. This assessment should consider factors such as their motivations, loyalty, reliability, and ability to access sensitive information.

Once potential agents have been identified, the next step is to establish contact with them and begin building a relationship. This process can take time and requires a great deal of patience, as it involves developing trust and mutual respect between the recruiter and the potential agent.

The first step Is to make initial contact, which can be done through a variety of methods such as a phone call, email, or face-to-face meeting. The recruiter must be prepared to introduce themselves and explain the purpose of the contact in a clear and concise manner. It is important to be honest and straightforward, as any attempt to deceive or manipulate the potential agent will likely lead to failure.

Once contact has been made, the recruiter must work to establish a relationship with the potential agent. This can involve regular communication, such as phone calls, emails, or face-to-face meetings, and may include sharing personal stories or experiences to build a sense of connection. The recruiter must also listen carefully to the potential agent and show genuine interest in their opinions and concerns.

It Is important to note that this process can take time, and the potential agent may require multiple interactions before they feel comfortable sharing sensitive information. The recruiter must be patient and persistent, while also being respectful of the potential agent's boundaries and concerns. Over time, a relationship of trust and mutual respect can be established, and the potential agent may become more willing to share sensitive information or consider working as an informant.

Before recruiting someone as an agent, it is important to screen and assess their qualifications, reliability, and loyalty. This involves conducting background checks, reviewing their personal and professional history, and evaluating their motivations and potential risks.

One common method of screening is through reference checks, which involves contacting individuals who know the potential agent and can vouch for their character and trustworthiness. It is also important to evaluate their technical skills and ability to handle sensitive information.

Another important aspect of assessing potential agents is evaluating their motivations and potential risks. Agents may be motivated by financial gain, ideological beliefs, or personal relationships. It is important to ensure that the agent's motivations align with the goals of the intelligence agency and that they are not susceptible to coercion or blackmail.

Thorough screening and assessment of potential agents is critical to ensure that the agency is able to recruit reliable and trustworthy individuals who can effectively carry out their duties.

Once an agent is recruited, it is essential to handle and manage them effectively to ensure their safety and success in their mission. The handler is responsible for overseeing the activities of the agent, including communication, reporting, and providing resources to carry out their tasks.

Communication is a critical aspect of agent management. The handler must establish secure channels of communication with the agent to ensure that their messages are not intercepted by the adversary. The handler should also maintain regular contact with the agent to provide guidance, support, and feedback on their performance.

The handler must also ensure that the agent has the necessary resources to carry out their tasks. This could include equipment, money, or other forms of support. The handler must maintain an inventory of these resources and ensure that they are delivered to the agent as needed.

Agent safety is paramount, and the handler must take all necessary measures to ensure that the agent is not compromised or exposed. This could include changing the agent's identity, location, or mission parameters as needed. The handler must also have contingency plans in place in case the agent is compromised, captured, or killed.

The handler must also maintain a detailed record of the agent's activities, including their reporting and any significant events or incidents. This record is essential for assessing the agent's performance and providing feedback and support.

Effective agent management requires trust, discretion, and attention to detail. The handler must be proactive and adaptable, responding to changes in the agent's environment and mission objectives. The handler's role is critical in ensuring the success of the agent's mission and protecting their safety and security.

Chapter 8: MICE

MICE is an acronym used to represent four categories of vulnerabilities that can be exploited in order to recruit an agent. The first category is money, which refers to the financial incentives that can be offered to a potential recruit in order to gain their loyalty and cooperation. This could include offering a large sum of money upfront, a regular salary or bonuses, or financial support for their family or other personal needs.

M stands for Money. This refers to financial incentives that may motivate an individual to betray their organization or country. Money is often a powerful motivator for espionage activities and can take various forms, such as cash payments, bonuses, or promises of future rewards. Money can be particularly attractive to those who feel underpaid or undervalued in their current position, or who are experiencing financial difficulties.

Espionage organizations often use financial incentives as a way to recruit potential agents. For example, they may target individuals with access to valuable information and offer them a significant sum of money in exchange for that information. Alternatively, they may identify individuals who are vulnerable to financial pressure, such as those with large debts or expensive habits, and use this vulnerability to blackmail them into cooperating. In some cases, intelligence agencies may also create fake companies or fronts to launder money and conceal their activities.

The "I" in the MICE acronym stands for "Ideology". This refers to an individual's beliefs, values, and principles. Ideology is a powerful motivator for individuals, as it is closely tied to a person's identity and sense of purpose. Those with strong ideological beliefs may be more willing to engage in espionage or other illegal activities if they feel it aligns with their values.

When recruiting individuals with a strong ideological motivation, intelligence agencies will often look for people who are passionate about a cause or belief system, and who are willing to take risks to advance that cause. This may include individuals involved in political or social activism, religious groups, or other organizations with a strong ideological bent.

Intelligence agencies will often use these ideological beliefs as leverage when recruiting agents. For example, they may appeal to an individual's sense of patriotism or desire to make a difference in the world to convince them to work for the agency. Alternatively, they may use the threat of exposure or punishment to force individuals to act on behalf of the agency.

The "C" In the MICE acronym stands for "Coercion." Coercion involves using force, threats, or intimidation to extract information from an individual. It can be a highly effective method for obtaining information quickly, but it also carries a significant risk of negative consequences.

In the context of intelligence gathering, coercion may involve physical violence or the threat of violence, such as torture or the use of other forms of physical force. It can also involve psychological pressure, such as threatening the subject's family, friends, or livelihood, or using other forms of psychological manipulation.

Coercion is a highly controversial method of intelligence gathering, and is generally viewed as unethical and illegal under international law. Many intelligence agencies have strict policies prohibiting the use of coercion, and may face legal consequences if they are caught engaging in such practices.

Despite these risks, some intelligence agencies continue to use coercion as a method of gathering information, often citing national security concerns as justification. However, in many cases, the information obtained through coercion may be unreliable, as subjects may be willing to say anything to stop the pain or threats.

Overall, the use of coercion as an intelligence gathering technique remains highly controversial, and should be approached with caution and careful consideration of the potential ethical and legal implications. Other, less coercive methods of intelligence gathering, such as surveillance and social engineering, may be more effective in many cases, and are generally considered to be more ethical and legal.

Ego is the fourth part in the MICE acronym, and it refers to appealing to the ego or personal motivations of a potential agent or asset. This is often done by offering incentives or appealing to an individual's sense of importance or desire for recognition. Ego-based recruiting can be effective, especially when dealing with individuals who have a strong sense of self-worth or who may be motivated by financial gain or a desire for power.

Ego-based recruitment techniques can include offering financial rewards, access to exclusive events or information, or the opportunity to gain a position of power or influence. In some cases, flattery or appeals to a person's vanity may also be effective. However, it's important to note that ego-based recruitment can also be risky, as individuals who are motivated primarily by their own self-interest may be more likely to betray or deceive those who recruited them.

To be successful in ego-based recruiting, it's important to carefully assess the motivations and personality of the target individual and tailor your approach accordingly. Building a rapport with the individual and establishing trust is also critical, as is being able to offer tangible benefits and incentives that align with the individual's personal goals and desires.

Chapter 9: Surveillance

Surveillance is the act of observing and monitoring the activities, behavior, or movements of a target or group of targets. It is an essential intelligence gathering technique used to obtain information about an individual, group, or organization. Surveillance can be conducted using various techniques, such as physical surveillance, technical surveillance, and electronic surveillance. The goal of surveillance is to collect information without being detected, which requires a high level of expertise and training. In this section, we will discuss the different types of surveillance techniques and how they are used in intelligence gathering.

Another important aspect of surveillance is understanding the environment. Before starting any surveillance operation, it's crucial to conduct a thorough reconnaissance of the area to identify potential hiding spots, escape routes, and blind spots. This can be done through various methods, such as walking around the area, studying maps and aerial photos, or even using advanced technology like drones or satellite imagery.

During the reconnaissance phase, it's also important to assess the potential risks and challenges that might arise during the operation. For instance, are there any security cameras or guards that might detect the surveillance team? Are there any natural obstacles like rivers or mountains that might make it difficult to track the target? Answering these questions can help the team prepare for any contingencies and ensure a successful operation.

In addition to the physical environment, the team must also consider the social environment. This means understanding the target's behavior, routines, and habits. By studying the target's schedule and identifying potential patterns, the team can increase their chances of capturing useful information or even catching the target in the act.

In addition to physical surveillance, there is also technical surveillance, which involves the use of electronic devices to gather information. This can include wiretapping phones, hacking into computers, or placing bugs in a target's location. Technical surveillance can be extremely useful in gathering information that might be difficult to obtain through physical surveillance, but it also carries a greater risk of discovery and legal consequences. Intelligence officers must carefully weigh the benefits and risks before using these techniques. It's important to note that the use of technical surveillance methods is heavily regulated and requires legal authorization in most countries.

There are various types of surveillance techniques that are employed by intelligence officers to gather information about their target. These techniques can be broadly classified into two categories: physical surveillance and technical surveillance.

Physical surveillance involves the use of human operatives to observe and track the movements of a target. This can be done either overtly or covertly. Overt surveillance is conducted openly, without attempting to conceal the fact that the target is being monitored. Covert surveillance, on the other hand, is done discreetly, without the knowledge of the target.

Technical surveillance, also known as electronic surveillance, involves the use of technological devices to intercept and record communications, and to monitor the activities of a target. This can include the use of wiretaps, bugs, cameras, and other forms of electronic eavesdropping.

It Is important for intelligence officers to carefully consider the type of surveillance technique that they will use, as well as the legal and ethical implications of their actions. For example, physical surveillance may be more effective in certain situations, but it also carries a higher risk of detection and potential legal consequences. Technical surveillance, while more discreet, may also be more limited in its scope and may require legal authorization before it can be conducted.

The analysis of data collected through surveillance should Involve identifying patterns, relationships, and connections between the data points. This could include identifying the subject's associates, their patterns of behavior, the places they frequent, and their mode of transportation. The analysis should be systematic, logical, and methodical to ensure that all the information is considered.

One of the essential things to consider during analysis is the reliability of the information. Intelligence officers must assess the information's accuracy and its sources to determine its reliability. This is critical because it can affect the entire operation's success or failure.

Overall, the process of analyzing the gathered information is critical in surveillance operations. A thorough analysis can provide valuable insights into the subject's behavior, their patterns, and their potential intentions.

Chapter 10: Escape and Evasion

Escape and evasion (E&E) is an essential skill for intelligence operatives who may need to operate in hostile environments or find themselves in dangerous situations. E&E is the art of avoiding capture and returning to friendly territory or completing the mission objective without being caught. It involves a range of techniques, from evading surveillance to eluding pursuit, and requires a combination of physical and mental preparation, as well as practical skills.

In the intelligence field, operatives often work in high-risk environments, and the risk of being captured or compromised is always present. The ability to escape and evade successfully can mean the difference between mission success and failure, or even life and death. As such, it is crucial for intelligence operatives to have a thorough understanding of E&E techniques and to train regularly to maintain these skills.

Throughout this chapter, we will explore various aspects of E&E, including planning and preparation, physical fitness and mental fortitude, and practical techniques for evasion and escape. By the end of this chapter, you will have a solid understanding of the importance of E&E for intelligence operatives and the key principles and techniques required to master this skillset.

In order to be successful, an intelligence operative must have a good understanding of their surroundings and the potential threats they may face. This means being aware of the local geography, terrain, climate, and infrastructure. They must also be able to quickly assess and adapt to changes in their environment. For example, if a city suddenly goes on lockdown due to a terrorist attack, the operative must be able to quickly change their plans and find a new route to safety. Additionally, the operative must be aware of the cultural norms and customs of the area they are operating in, as well as any language barriers that may hinder communication. By having a thorough understanding of their surroundings, an intelligence operative can increase their chances of successfully evading capture and reaching safety.

Once an intelligence operative has found themselves in a dangerous or compromised situation, their priority should be to identify potential escape and evasion routes. This requires prior planning and knowledge of the area, including understanding the local terrain, road systems, and transportation infrastructure.

When identifying escape and evasion routes, it is important to consider the fastest and safest routes to get out of the area, while avoiding heavily monitored areas, checkpoints, or areas that may be controlled by hostile forces. Intelligence operatives must also have contingency plans in place in case their primary escape routes are blocked or compromised.

The ability to Identify escape and evasion routes is essential to the success of any intelligence operation. It is therefore important for operatives to continually assess their environment and have a deep understanding of the local area to ensure they can navigate and identify potential escape routes quickly and effectively.

Navigation is a crucial skill in escape and evasion, especially in unfamiliar terrain. Intelligence operatives need to be able to navigate through urban or rural areas, forests, mountains, and other types of landscapes without getting lost. They should know how to use a map, compass, and GPS, and be able to read the terrain to find the safest and most efficient routes to their destination. They also need to know how to navigate using the stars, sun, or moon, in case they lose access to their tools or the GPS signal is lost. Without proper navigation skills, an operative risks getting lost, which could result in being captured or killed. Therefore, mastering navigation skills is essential for any intelligence operative who might need to escape and evade in a hostile environment.

In an escape and evasion situation, it's essential to avoid detection by those who may be looking for you. This can be done by using natural cover, such as bushes, trees, and rocks, to stay hidden and out of sight. It's important to keep moving and avoid staying in one location for too long, as this increases the risk of being discovered.

When moving, try to keep a low profile, avoid making noise, and stay away from open areas where you may be easily spotted. If possible, stick to back alleys, side streets, and other less traveled areas. If you have to cross open terrain, do so quickly and at a time when you're less likely to be seen, such as at night or during inclement weather.

If you're being pursued, you may need to take more drastic measures to avoid detection. These can include changing your appearance by altering your clothing, cutting your hair, or using makeup to change your facial features. You may also need to use decoys or diversionary tactics to draw your pursuers away from your location and give yourself time to escape.

Overall, avoiding detection is a critical element of escape and evasion, and it requires quick thinking, good situational awareness, and the ability to adapt to changing circumstances.

To successfully execute escape and evasion techniques, an intelligence operative must possess practical skills that can be used in a variety of situations. Some of these skills include:

Navigation: Knowing how to read a map and use a compass is essential for finding one's way in unfamiliar terrain.

First aid: Being able to treat injuries and illnesses in the field can be the difference between life and death.

Shelter building: Knowing how to construct a shelter to protect oneself from the elements is important for survival in extreme environments.

Fire building: The ability to start a fire is critical for staying warm, cooking food, and purifying water.

Stealth and concealment: Knowing how to move quietly and hide oneself from view can help an operative avoid detection.

Self-defense: Being able to protect oneself from physical harm may be necessary in hostile situations.

By developing these practical skills, an intelligence operative can increase their chances of survival and successful evasion in the field. It is important for operatives to regularly train and hone these skills to maintain their proficiency.

Chapter 11: Surveillance Detection Routes

Surveillance detection routes (SDRs) are an essential tool in the toolbox of any intelligence operative. These routes are specifically designed to help individuals identify and avoid surveillance by hostile actors who may be tracking their movements. Whether an operative is conducting an operation, meeting with a contact, or simply going about their daily routine, it is critical to be able to detect and evade any attempts to monitor their activities.

SDRs are carefully planned and executed routes that are designed to make it difficult for surveillance teams to keep up with the operative. The routes may involve taking a variety of transportation modes, using different entrances and exits, and incorporating stops at various locations to break up the operative's movements. The goal of an SDR is to make it difficult for any potential surveillance team to maintain visual or physical contact with the operative.

An effective SDR requires a deep understanding of the operational environment, including knowledge of the local terrain, transportation systems, and potential surveillance threats. It also requires a clear understanding of the operative's objectives, schedule, and personal habits. With this information, the operative can plan a route that incorporates specific measures designed to detect and evade surveillance.

The benefits of SDRs are clear. By successfully avoiding surveillance, the operative can maintain operational security, protect their personal safety, and increase the likelihood of achieving their objectives. In addition, SDRs can serve as a critical tool for identifying and disrupting hostile surveillance activities. By recognizing and responding to surveillance attempts, the operative can take steps to counter the threat and protect their mission.

The purpose of a surveillance detection route is to identify if an individual or organization is being followed or surveilled by an adversary. The key to a successful surveillance detection route is to blend in with the surroundings and appear as a regular part of the environment, so as not to arouse suspicion.

To begin, it's important to have a clear understanding of the area and route to be covered. This may include identifying possible surveillance threats, such as static or mobile surveillance. Once these threats are identified, a route can be planned that incorporates a variety of techniques to help detect surveillance.

One technique used in surveillance detection routes is the use of landmarks. Landmarks are physical points on the route that can be used as reference points to identify any deviations from the planned path. These landmarks can be anything from buildings or statues to street signs or trees, as long as they are distinct enough to stand out from the surrounding environment.

To create a surveillance detection route, you first need to identify the potential surveillance points in your area. These points can be anything from street corners to parked cars, and they will vary depending on the specific environment you are in. Once you have identified these points, you will need to determine the most effective route to take that avoids them.

When designing a surveillance detection route, there are several factors to consider. You want to avoid taking the same route every day, as this will make you predictable and easier to follow. Instead, you should vary your route and take different paths each time. You should also avoid walking too quickly or too slowly, as this can make you stand out and draw attention to yourself.

It's also Important to pay attention to your surroundings while you're on the route. Look for anything unusual or out of place, such as people or vehicles that seem to be following you or appear to be parked in the same spot every day. Make note of these observations and report them to your intelligence agency, so they can take appropriate action.

Another key aspect of surveillance detection routes is maintaining situational awareness. This means being aware of your surroundings and paying attention to any potential threats or danger. It's important to stay alert and focused, even while you're on a familiar route, as complacency can make you vulnerable to surveillance.

Once the initial route has been planned, the operative should execute it multiple times to gain familiarity and identify any potential issues. This will also help in refining the route and ensuring its efficiency.

During the execution of the route, the operative should constantly scan the surroundings for any potential surveillance, paying attention to people or vehicles that seem to be following them. They should also pay attention to any potential choke points or areas where they may be vulnerable to attack.

It Is also important to use the elements of surprise and unpredictability when executing the route. This means varying the route, speed, and mode of transportation, as well as changing the time and day of execution to prevent the surveillance team from predicting their movements.

Additionally, the operative should have a contingency plan in case they identify a surveillance team. This could involve seeking cover or entering a safe location, such as a crowded area or a police station. The operative should also have the necessary equipment, such as a covert communication device, to contact their support team in case of an emergency.

An important step in executing a surveillance detection route is to have a plan in place for when you detect surveillance. This is a critical component of the process as it allows you to react quickly and effectively if you believe that you are being followed. You should always have a plan for what to do if you suspect that you are under surveillance, including where to go, who to contact, and how to communicate with them. It is important to have a contingency plan in case your primary plan is compromised or fails.

In order to have an effective plan, it is essential to have a thorough understanding of your surroundings and the various routes that you can take to evade potential surveillance. This includes knowledge of the local area, such as the location of police stations, hospitals, and other public places where you can seek refuge or assistance. It is also important to have a basic understanding of the transportation infrastructure, such as bus and train routes, as well as the location of taxi stands and car rental facilities.

In addition, it is crucial to have a network of trusted individuals who can provide assistance in the event of an emergency or suspected surveillance. This network may include family members, friends, colleagues, or other individuals who can offer support and guidance. It is important to have a plan in place for communicating with these individuals, including specific protocols for how to contact them and what information to provide.

It's vital when executing an SDR to maintain situational awareness and assess potential threats. This involves staying alert and observant of any changes or abnormalities in your surroundings. By doing so, you can identify any potential threats and respond accordingly.

To maintain situational awareness, use all of your senses to gather information about your environment. Listen for sounds that seem out of place, such as footsteps or the sound of a car engine that seems to be following you. Look for anything that seems unusual or out of the ordinary, such as a person who appears to be watching you or a vehicle that seems to be parked in an unusual location. Use your sense of smell to detect any strange or unusual odors, such as the smell of gasoline or exhaust fumes.

Another important aspect of maintaining situational awareness is to be aware of your own behavior. Avoid doing anything that might draw attention to yourself or make you stand out from the crowd. For example, don't stop and stare at something for an extended period of time, or walk in a way that draws attention to yourself. Instead, blend in with your surroundings and act as If you belong there.

If you do identify a potential threat, the key is to act quickly and decisively. This may involve altering your route, changing your appearance, or seeking out a safe location where you can call for help. It's important to remember that the goal of an SDR is to detect and avoid potential threats, not to confront them head-on. By staying alert and aware, and by responding quickly and effectively to potential threats, you can successfully execute an SDR and minimize your risk of detection.

Chapter 12: Disguise

Disguise and blending in with the surroundings are crucial skills for intelligence operatives, as they enable them to move around unnoticed and gather information without attracting unwanted attention. The ability to blend in with the surroundings is particularly important in situations where the operative is operating in a hostile environment, where any indication of their presence could lead to immediate danger. Disguise, on the other hand, allows the operative to take on a new identity, making it more difficult for their adversaries to identify them.

The art of disguise has been used for centuries, dating back to ancient times when warriors used it as a means of gaining an advantage over their enemies. Today, the use of disguise has become more sophisticated, with intelligence agencies employing skilled professionals who are able to change their appearance, mannerisms, and even their accent to blend in seamlessly with their environment. In this chapter, we will explore the techniques used by intelligence operatives to disguise themselves and blend in with their surroundings.

The goal is to be able to move around unnoticed and gather information without drawing attention to oneself. A good disguise can help an operative to blend in with their surroundings and avoid detection. In this section, we will discuss the basics of disguise and blending in, including how to choose appropriate clothing and accessories, how to alter physical appearance, and how to act in a way that is consistent with the environment.

When choosing clothing and accessories, the operative must take into consideration the surroundings and the culture of the area. Clothing that is too flashy or out of place can draw attention and make the operative stand out. Accessories like hats, sunglasses, and scarves can help to conceal facial features and draw attention away from the face. It is important to choose accessories that are appropriate for the environment and blend in with the local style. For example, wearing a baseball cap in a formal setting would be out of place and draw attention.

In addition to clothing and accessories, altering physical appearance can be an effective way to disguise oneself. This can include changing hair color or style, growing or shaving facial hair, or using makeup to create a different look. However, it is important to be aware of cultural norms and not do anything that would be considered offensive or disrespectful. For example, in some cultures, women wearing makeup may be considered inappropriate or disrespectful.

Overall, the key to effective disguise and blending in is to be aware of the surroundings and culture, and to make choices that are appropriate and consistent with the environment. In the following sections, we will discuss these concepts in more detail and provide tips and techniques for successful disguise and blending in.

Before attempting to blend in with the surroundings, it is important to assess the environment carefully. This means taking note of the types of people who are present, their behaviors, dress, and mannerisms. This can be done from a distance, or up close by mingling with the crowd. It is important to take note of the local customs and traditions and make sure to blend in accordingly. This can be done by observing the way locals dress and behave in public, as well as the way they interact with each other. Additionally, it is important to be aware of any cultural taboos or sensitive subjects that should be avoided.

In addition to observing the people, it is also important to assess the physical surroundings. This includes taking note of the architecture, the landscaping, and any other notable features. This will help in identifying areas that provide good opportunities for blending in, as well as areas to avoid. It is also important to pay attention to the traffic flow and movement patterns, as this will help in identifying potential escape routes or areas to avoid.

In addition to changing appearance, using props is another technique for creating a convincing disguise. Props can be anything from a briefcase to a walking stick to a shopping bag, depending on the environment and the character being portrayed. Props can help an operative blend in with their surroundings and create a more natural appearance.

When selecting props, it's important to choose items that are consistent with the character's story and environment. For example, if the operative is posing as a businessman, a briefcase would be a common and appropriate prop. However, if the operative is in a beach town, a briefcase would be out of place and could draw attention.

Another consideration is how the prop is used. If the prop is something that is normally carried, it should be held and used naturally to avoid suspicion. If the prop is something that is not normally carried, the operative should be careful to avoid drawing too much attention to it.

There are various types of disguises that can be used by intelligence operatives to blend in with their surroundings. These include:

Physical disguises: This involves changing the physical appearance of the agent, such as through the use of wigs, makeup, fake facial hair, and prosthetics.

Clothing disguises: Agents can blend in with their surroundings by dressing appropriately for the environment. For example, if they are in a beach area, they can dress in casual clothing and carry beach items.

Cultural disguises: This involves adopting the local culture of the area. The agent may change their accent or dialect, adopt local customs, and even change their name.

Psychological disguises: Agents can use psychological disguises to blend in with their surroundings. This involves acting as if they belong in the area, using appropriate body language, and engaging in conversation with locals.

The type of disguise used will depend on the situation and environment the agent is in. A well-planned and executed disguise can make all the difference in the success of an intelligence operation.

To make a disguise more convincing, intelligence operatives often create a believable backstory that they can use if questioned. This backstory includes details such as their name, occupation, place of birth, and other personal information. It is important to create a backstory that is both believable and easy to remember, so that it can be recalled quickly and naturally if needed.

When creating a backstory, the operative must also take into consideration the context of the situation they are in. For example, if they are infiltrating a business, they may want to create a backstory that involves working in a similar industry. If they are posing as a tourist, they may want to research popular tourist attractions in the area and create a backstory around that.

The backstory should also include information about the operative's current activities and plans, which should be consistent with their cover story. For example, if the operative is posing as a tourist, their plans for the day should involve visiting popular tourist attractions, not attending secret meetings.

Creating a believable backstory requires careful research and planning, but it can be a powerful tool for blending in and avoiding suspicion. A well-crafted backstory can help an operative navigate tricky situations and maintain their cover, ultimately increasing the chances of a successful mission.

As with any skill, effective disguise and blending in require practice and training. Intelligence operatives undergo extensive training to learn the techniques of disguise and blending in, including practice in real-life scenarios.

One effective training technique is to have operatives blend in with a crowd in a public place, such as a busy shopping center or train station, and try to avoid being detected by a designated observer. This exercise helps operatives learn how to adjust their behavior and appearance to blend in with their surroundings and avoid drawing attention to themselves.

Operatives also practice creating and wearing disguises, using a variety of materials to alter their appearance and become unrecognizable. They may practice altering their hair, makeup, clothing, and even their posture and gait to become someone entirely different.

By regularly practicing and training in these techniques, intelligence operatives can improve their ability to blend in and remain unnoticed, even in high-risk situations.

Conclusion:

As you reach the end of Essential Spycraft, you have gained a glimpse into the world of intelligence gathering and the skills necessary to succeed in this field. Whether you aspire to become a spy, work in law enforcement, or just want to learn new skills, the techniques covered in this book provide a foundation for success.

Remember, the techniques in this book are not just for spies; they can be applied to many different situations where observation, analysis, and quick thinking are necessary. You never know when you might need to blend in with your surroundings or evade detection, so it's always best to be prepared.

Above all, the world of intelligence gathering is not just about gadgets and fancy gadgets, but also about the human element. It's about understanding people, their motivations, and their vulnerabilities. The skills you've learned in this book will help you not only in the world of espionage but in everyday life as well.

So go forth and use your new skills with confidence and responsibility. Whether you're a spy or a civilian, always remember to stay vigilant and stay safe.